HOMAGE TO HENRY ALLINE
& OTHER POEMS

Books by Douglas Lochhead

Poetry

The Heart is Fire (1959)
It is All Around (1960)
Poet Speaking (1964)
A&B&C&: An Alphabet (1969)
Millwood Road Poems (1970)
Prayers in a Field (1974)
Collected Poems: The Full Furnace (1975)
High Marsh Road (1980)
battle sequence (1980)
A&E (1980)
The Panic Field (1984)
Tiger in the Skull: New and Selected Poems (1986)
Upper Cape Poems (1989)
Dykelands (with photographs by Thaddeus Holownia, 1989)
Black Festival (1991)

HOMAGE to HENRY ALLINE

& OTHER POEMS

DOUGLAS LOCHHEAD

GOOSE LANE

Some of the poems in this book have appeared previously in the following journals: *The Antigonish Review*: 'Vigils & Mercies,' 'Elegies 1-10'; *The Dalhousie Review*: 'Homage to Henry Alline,' parts I-XIV; also in *Upper Cape Poems*, Goose Lane Editions, 1989, parts I-XIV.

Published with the assistance of the Canada Council and the New Brunswick Department of Municipalities, Culture and Housing, 1992.

Book design by Julie Scriver and Douglas Lochhead.
Printed in Canada by the Tribune Press.
10 9 8 7 6 5 4 3 2

Canadian Cataloguing in Publication Data

Lochhead, Douglas, 1922 -
    Homage to Henry Alline and other poems
    ISBN 0-86492-125-X

I. Title.

PS8523.O33H66 1992   C811'.54   C92-098569-6
PR9199.3.L63H66 1992

Goose Lane Editions
469 King Street
Fredericton, New Brunswick
Canada E3B 1E5

Contents

Foreword

Henry Alline was born in Newport, Rhode Island on 14 June 1748. He died at North Hampton, New Hampshire on 2 February 1784 of consumption. After moving with his family to Nova Scotia he left life on the farm to become an itinerant evangelical preacher. Self-educated and driven by his revivalistic passion he spent most of his life as a saddle-bag preacher in Nova Scotia and New Brunswick. Henry Alline was a tireless traveller and speaker. Miraculously he also managed to write a number of significant theological works including *Two Mites on Some of the Most Important and Much Disputed Points of Divinity* (1781), *Hymns and Spiritual Songs* (1786) and his *Life and Journal* (1806). The above works, particularly his *Life and Journal*, have, in large measure, provided the inspiration for *Homage to Henry Alline*.

This might well be called a poem for voices. Three voices. First there is the historian throwing in his hard-won details to provide background. Second, in *italics*, there is Henry himself speaking so eloquently in passages taken from his *Journal and his Hymns*. And finally there is the occasional sound from the present in the form of questions which are the poet's.

The source of this somewhat chronological sequence of poems is Henry Alline as he emerges in his own writings and in those scholars who have written about him. There is also, inevitably, something of myself. The

poems are meant to be a celebration. A tribute, an act
of homage, to a man of God. To some extent it is a
dialogue between Henry and a contemporary voice.
Some questions and answers. Henry Alline would have
been uneasy with the celebration but would have
welcomed the dialogue. *His* time and *this* time are *one*
time as far as Alline was concerned. It was always the
eternal Now. All those glorious noises from the great lap
of sky which were his from that day and night of his
conversion in 1775 until he died, if he did die, in 1784.

To Henry Alline and his writings — the *Journal,*
the hymns, the tracts — I acknowledge my debt first
and foremost. Many lines of his appear in italics in the
text. It was in William James' *The Varieties of Religious
Experience* that I was first introduced to Henry Alline
when I was an undergraduate at McGill in 1942. Later
I read Alline as interpreted by George A. Rawlyk, in
particular, and by Maurice W. Armstrong, Gordon
Stewart, Jack M. Bumsted, James Beverley and Barry
Moody. To the historians I offer my thanks for their
points of view. But the poems offered here are largely
Henry's. I have taken from his vision (how steadfast that
is), and endeavoured to frame parts with my own
commentary of selected colours.

DL

I

Homage to Henry Alline

I

Dog did bark. Cattle slushed in their places.
An elm cracked high in its flaked branches.
Blood on the back step. Someone hacked in a craze
of death. I was awake to it. Me. Henry. Savages.
But they did not come. Or did they? No. It was
a dream-shock. God and myself. Hog-reeves
and pound-keepers, fence-viewers from Halifax.
Larking about.

II

For Sunday. Hair in a queue. Barefoot boy
given to frolics. Fiddle-play and a dance or two.
Black-edge guilt frames the Falmouth shore.
I turn inward. Hymn for one. God
in a place. Set me down.

III

Fountain. Source. Glory. Angelic realms.
Reach for words. Showers. Dead leaves.
Some as birds of magnificent colours.
What is my theme? You ask. *His name*
should be my theme. Until the last period
of my days. Me. My own censor.
Your horse, Henry. What about your horse?

IV

Once sun-colours. The Gaspereaux.
Black and white are my thoughts. Words.
Shaped doings. Lightning in my crib.
Then straight down to darkness.
I stood on the brink. Like the song.
I remember it well.
Out of bed holding hatred
for the grinning, sinning Adam.

V

Heebie-jeebie world. Given over
to Big Gruesome. Last night larking.
Why are you and all the rest
like hopped-up Adams? Numb with questions.
Crouched in the attic.
Waded through pools of pity. Who
can spell mercy? The blood-let garden.
Nine at the time, was Henry. Still questions.
The loving, good God dresses
in city, sweating jeans? With no blanket of mercy?
Where is God's tongue?

VI

Speak and write as child. DEATH
is my tossing-time. Fear. Dying. Going.
All atremble. Swimming. Side-stroke
in shallow places. Foot on bottom.
I pray while my arms flounder.
Prayers leave me like limp sparrows
waiting to be plucked by the great Hand.

VII

Today the field is my place. Thoughts
stick to burdocks. Birds are wind-hurt.
Bobolinks startle in daisy grasses. Song on metal.
Crow. Still as death. I look into branches.
Horton's elms. Mass of thoughts
blowing me into a state. What matter.
He seems to know.

VIII

I did read and study much. Great.
Bunyon, Milton, maybe? My Meccano
was a veritable Babel. It stood.
The devil's back, my footings.
Grand conceit. My wave to eternity.
Unfathomable eternity. Close on to mystery.

IX

Key words. Unhappiness. Torment.
My *Journal* revels. Devil tells me.
A little mad I was. No annihilation.
Please. Funny God. Me the goodie-goodie.
Wailing, leaping, stopping and turning times.
Crazy doll. I unwind into a ball.
O Lord, mercy, etc.

X

O the subtlety of the grand adversary!
Letters of His Law. Night sweat.
I had seen her before but had
no great acquaintance with. Will
not go! No horse could drag me.
Into her arms. Erase thoughts, words.
No deeds. Henry, speaking of a horse . . .

XI

Down by Payzants. Black land.
Scotched hemlock. Birch, Juniper, Pine.
Foreground of weeping plants. Lambskill.
Swamp laurel. Leather leaf. All this
a place, a fore and background
for my laid-out soul. Mouth mercy.
Inside shout. I am no pleaser.

XII

No tools. Chisel. Hammer
unchipped rock face. I am human.
Blood slow. Red cross in red stone.
My hacked-away thanks. Raised beach.
Hard. Words. Caught in the roll of tide.
Feet show. The cross in dark shadow
where the beach stays. Tide snorts.
A doubting song.

XIII

New lights. Parlour game. Let's play.
Jennie fall on floor and froth.
We'll all wail. Voices. Someone will give
running commentary of his/her indecencies.
O Abigail. Don't go. You will be taken.
O Lord rebuke me not in thy wrath.

XIV

Substantial food and settled joy.
I play with the psalms. 38, 40.
My eyes find white lights. White
fields. Trees. The sky is festival.
Enough. Enough. All this in one half hour.
Now I am pointed His Way.
Me. Labourer. Old folk retired.
Red mud on the boots. Unworthy worm.
Worm.

XV

April 13th, 14th? 1776. Why, I ask, do I need
to qualify for Christ? He will graduate me.
Should I speak? Through opening spring woods I went.
Time to see tongues of new growth
leaping from His every tree. Like happy snakes.
The Lord told me to preach. This I did on Sabbath.
It was not easy. Parents. Strange strings of tension
working the knees. Feet a constant tangle.
If thou art wise, thou art wise for myself,
but if thou scornest, thou alone shall bear it.

XVI

Something of a curiosity. A card. Many came
from other towns. Boat loads. I, Henry,
was a booming babbler. Some said they were glad
I had begun. Others could not take it.
Parents found me too much. But they hung around.
Bold I was and full of noise and music.
Preached twice on Sunday. Wrought with my hands
all week. Some sad are one-day swallows.
Wild torn stitches of life. I am tied to Him.

XVII

Looking out. Was it Horton, Falmouth? God knows.
With Him it is Now. Who runs? Who walks?
Standing is running into itself. *He said let us*
make Man, and the Sound of the last Trumpet,
in the same instant . . . Death is Birth . . . Now.
There is One. It is Eternity. Eternal eyes
seeing across the glittering Bay, into it
and into ourselves. The Great Eye. The Great Now.
Yes, it was Falmouth. I know it was.
A Payzant looked after my horse.

XVIII

Ah me. Forgive. For I look into the blackness
of myself. Henry's pit. It can be no other.
Only the wish (it will come) of a crazy spark
to kindle the wreck and spindrift of my soul.
My horse limps. Like that for hours. He goes
with me, always uphill, into my darker spaces.
Foot places he would never have dared to go.
God rides beside, inside. Around us good plants
for eating — wood sorrel, cinnamon fern, lamb's quarters,
sow thistle, wild rose, shepherd's purse.
We sit and rest it out. Me, Henry, you asked.
Now pray for me and my nameless horse.

XIX

I speak to you. You to me. There is no stop
and go. It is now. Sound there a bell.
My ears ring with it and unexpected prayers.
One to fill the rafters in Cornwallis, Yarmouth,
Sackfield, all the places God's map shows.
There is a forever flame. Did I tell you?
That night I opened a bedroom door. Someone
breathing, listening, waiting. We lay in a sweat
of ecstasy, in a tumbled shower of arms not words.
God's will. I talked and no sound came.
Henry was all I heard and slept, I did,
on a kitchen couch. This all came back to me.
Blinding, black story. My own heart-sick phoenix.

XX

Neither Succession nor Progress . . .
let us make Man, and the sound of last Trumpets
(That glorious signal and angel-chime)
is the very same instant . . . with God all things
are now as the Centre of a Ring . . .
That big Boom you are making joyful noise about, Henry.
And there was what followed the first apple bite.
No inch by bleeding inch for you Henry. You could be
   right.

XXI

July first, Joseph Bailey invited me
to speak at his house. Newport. Great numbers.
Bold and full of voice was I but looking down,
awash with words, there was disappointment
for those who came to watch my fall. He was/is
with me now and now. To go out and walk
taking in God's wonder. The trees, the few
are past their blossom and fruit will hang,
apples from his green sanctuary of garden. Here.
Winds off his beginning sea blow my hair.
It is a private presence there, slippers in sand.
His silvering creatures everywhere. I will
gather a visible church. Ordained two elders.

XXII

Twice preached at Horton. He is my pulpit,
my beautiful burning source. Many a frolic
I once had then. The people had hearing ears.
To Cornwallis, a late-year storm running
a pelting shiver of water on earth's bones.
My horse bent into it and came up lame. Again.
I changed him, rubbing down, whispering his name.
This year I remember Falmouth, the year's start.
Still the long conscience of my rousing youth
my wallowing in all manner of sin and vanity.
This new year explodes over Falmouth with a
happy congregation, I almost said conspiracy,
of stars. Outside the sea beams this night.
It is a time, as all times, for devotion to his praise.

XXIII

In a bath of dog-violets so I did pick one to see
God's face in this low fruit, five petals, some with
    purple veins
and it flowers from March to July they say. And *I*
    enjoyed what
the world knows nothing of. Me, amidst the violet
    glories.
Worm in the dust. Next day I did ride sixteen miles
where a popish priest kept silent at my sermon.
I ride a wider circuit yet the land is christian dark.
Sparks fizz in their hearts. Take Cornwallis
where I was shadowed by two ministers from Cobequid.
Offered me their libraries to go through before I
    preached
again. Would you believe they called me
a stiff young man? Me, Henry, stiff you say.

XXIV

Annapolis. Ripe fields. I look into the Lord's eye.
Henry, I must interrupt. Henry you are there
to sing. To sing the Lord's song. Henry, this is
what you are telling me. Your *Journal*. If we are
to know the Lord, we should know His song. Yes,
tell me: "the Lord is a singer and first his song
is a love-song. The work of creation is a song.
The morning stars sing together." A printer friend,
Henry, said that. He told me, "In a song
all things must sing."* Think of it, Henry.
You are the conductor. All of the strings
the world has shall be plucked. Shall be
run over and back by a thousand, shivering winds.

*Eric Gill *The Lord's Song*, 1934

XXV

My limping ways. Out of deeper waters voices
chase me into corners of dark. The fathomed soul
grows white again because the blackest nights
bring the brightest of His lights. How I do try
to keep my tongue as with a bridle. Lest my lips
grow hot, go wild. Then when they (for instance,
I remember Cornwallis and Londonderry)
have had their times at me I give ringing phrases
for all to hear. God loves. But I confess I grow
fed-up with those who cannot forget the water tricks.
My voice of God's which rings them round to go home
singing loud. Even in opposition do I find an ecstasy.

XXVI

A winter's time. Filled to the brim with birth,
the quiet hosannahs coming down the sky
from Blomidon. The scene from here is swaddling white.
Where animals stay in the hard-done yards
and there is the sun of celebration on the watching sea.
Now in the Falmouth barns they sing and pray,
mouthing their own passing hymns in the midst of
　　winter days.
Hosannahs to the Son of David.
And I could not shake free my troubled mind,
which seemed to forbade no good.
Is this the signal and the sign of the galloping
　　consumption?
Closer I feel to Jonah in hell's belly. These days and
　　nights
I went down to the bottom of mountains
and the earth with her bars was about me.

XXVII

Out of a deeper place I came up with His help.
Shouting great joy for I had been tested
and come through! Look, I say, come through!
Only to reach Cornwallis and God, thy people
cry out with small pox. The place is blackened.
Jacketed in darkness. In desolate fear.
March fever-winds blow bringing disbelief
masking the valley face. Dark train of weeping flesh.
And *every face a gathered blackness*.
Thy people wait and do not hear. Yet,
in all of this, I remember my deliverance.

XXVIII

Falmouth, a woman convicted, up to her knees
and beyond in temptations. So I did grapple
the Devil in her and I whipped him down.
More. Disaster. Mrs. G. with small pox. Hot with it.
We spoke together but in two days she was gone.
She to the glorious realms of light, as I call them.
O the trump of God and the happy wailings there.
I employ myself with writing this and given
God's song the hymns grow like roses in my mouth.
Almost at every writing their wondrous flowering
fills my soul as I wait. O the waiting
to meet the Lord in air. His words are there.

XXIX

Hot sun given to afternoon of clouds and warnings.
I sat out on the stoop of a house and saw a grand elm
of His own making come shattering down.
Struck by His flame of lightning just like that:
flaming sheets, blazing shock, bellowing thunder.
The burning scene, everlasting flame.
O, the great trials of mind go blowing through us
just as this day my sore throat, a swelling
quite bunged up except for liquids they poured
in me until I spoke. The goings of God in his sanctuary.
I jest (or do I ever?) now take the drunken drummer
dispatched to beat me down. Took wrong way
and missed both tavern and my session.

XXX

How I have limped over these past swelling days.
But now darkness has fallen away. Grand light
fills my eye-glass of sky. What is there now
but to make voice, abscess and all, my loud
and secret praises? I am sick with love.
Where are my friends? They need me not.
The horse fed, rubbed and shining
stays in the barn's warmth. The asthma
increases. So I gave a list of things to happen.
Go out to Glory tidy and all. I know my needs.
The creatured universe is a little song of love.
His love. And I would listen.

II

the ledge of winter

the ledge of winter:
while before us
a dog slips home
to where there are
fires

the white becomes black
early
the night
severs the voices
which sound from woods

it is all we can take

the ice cracks
up and down the river
we are to wait and see
it will be a matter of weeks
we were told this
the others agreed nodding
buttoning up
fastening snowshoes

for some it was their first
walk, so early,

the river being with ice
giving off steam
breathing at the mouth

Marsh prayers

1

Give God, your great lines
unfold. Give straight blood
in veins forgiven, the light
your vast lantern shows

to hay-bent scenes of snow
and ice, bring furious fire
and scar my tongue of all
my old tired diction given

the wind-long passages
of marsh undo, the heart
shrinks, give cheek
and body to the cold

Give God, to all things
crowns of minor glimmer
to shine as lights, as sparks,
over this flat kingdom.

2

Thy kingdom come
at last is here,
we dare not speak,
or do we dare?

fox, harrier, owl
and marsh-blown place,
the spun-spent clouds
hang wired in space

go down, come down
in fear-filled veins
to cool searing flesh
on these grieving plains

marsh fogs and frost
and antique nails
hold to these barns
thy gold-won bales.

3

Spin wide, spin strong
go with me now
your given place
your given bread

multitudes unleash
a grinning grave
a live song, wild song
on every face

spin-wide wild lines,
the sky's long page
takes them as streamers,
sentences of rage

black pilgrimages tell
of dry and darker eyes
the marsh road endures,
harriers take fire.

from kill to kill

into a twist
of wilderness

the puzzle
and game

where life
of panther paw

is deep stuck
driven there

to tell tales
of wilderness

as it is to us
going after

in blind fold
searching

what to it
the animal

is strong
and sure

going straight
and there

from kill to kill

Images

1

a black flag
stains
the hard blue
of sky

three crows
are it
and
it's flapping

2

now white
the page
is given
words

they lie
as fallen
things
waiting

for someone
to bandage
them
as poems

3

whose voice
but the wind
sings
the final song?

4

a bird
alerts
the snow
to fall
from branches

5

the fire
provides
an offering

its smell
touches
the town

there are
so many
messages

to be written
down
for later

6

the stone
in dry
winter

conceals
a warmth
of sand

as blood
which moves
through it

dry
breathing
winter-stone

7

under me
a drift
of ocean

warm crush
of centuries
in push & shove

the sand
outside
glimmers under palms

how is it
wildly
possible

all this
unaccountable
warmth?

8

a salvage
of winter
snow

a damage
of cold
surrounds;

a collapse
of storm
roars

but somehow
a welcome
coverup

comes
in a winter's
silence

this morning I went out

this morning I went out
and walked the imaginary beach
the long stretch just out there
where the field turns blue
and the sky is lighter above it.

It was a crowded place
of gulls, turnstones, plover,
all their quick skitter and cry
the earnest play
of their survival

then into it, the low surf,
a dream-wave crashing, a long lip
of turning, which meant
something in my own turning,
the eyes seemed no part of it

and to the red ripples of sand
as the wind shapes the Arctic snow
and it is a solid map for Innuit
but the rest of us are lost
so the ripples wave at last.

When, I think I remember, I walked
the same beach to see the growth
and wreckage of it, it was I think
more exciting to try its measure
its stretch of dream that time.

sprung

the spring filled brook
babbles a new song
a longer epic

and into each nudge
of root and rock
a bounce of white

of backyard lyrics
I hear through
a now silence

where stand hemlocks
nude birches and
a touch of poplar

the high-hole hammers
a love din
of bird-yearning

such is the sombre state
of spring come quickly
now to have a party

the innocent returned
the green glow
a forest watch and wake

new witnesses abound
in newer clothes
a beginning tangled garden

where brush recovers
from the storm and rasp-
berries break loose

it is a crow's place too
black with wings
they come and go as owners

it is not enough to say
even a rosy part of it
given what we know

it is the not knowing
that climbs aboard
our pulsing backs

You do agree I take it
have this and this
and yet again have this

what climbing urges
shape our feelings into needles
of the ancestral nag

so now I tell thee
on my speaking knees
let us endeavour to forget.

Elegies 1 – 10

1

there is always time
the blind clock
tells its singular song

you are always
within a grand distance

the tucked hand
contains
a timeless pulse

2

some report there are drums
but it is only the sea

only the breath and cough
of the world

the turning in bed-fathoms
making something happen

but who is to listen?
who is to care?

3

until the silence opens
then what stories to tell

who will listen then
my pretty hen?

no, a child goes slowly
and dies in the room

then there is silence
the deafness of death

4

now it is time
the sand grows cold

there is only a warmth
locked in two pebbles

given out for taking
from the black hand

5

there was once
a petal torn from flower

somewhere an act
small and monstrous as that

yet, in its colour
its own yellow softness

the petal changed all of it
into majestic ceremony

6

I told you the petal-story
and you seemed to hear

with head turning away
from death, a kind of delay

and I went away and dreamed
of the petal in your hair

7

how does the dance go on?
how do the dancers move?

the beach grips each foot
in its shift of sands

running seas push and wash
the dancers into strange ways

steps they never knew
as the tow takes them under
two by two

8

for a while we grew
by mountains, white

places, high tough peaks
as serious as we

who played in their shadows
picked roses in Christmas snows

coming as close as we could
as hawks to ground

but they were still there
the white mountains

so that spring we took fire
and fled from their dark

carrying our love-embers
to a new field, a new place

9

there must be sure things
as light on yellow leaves

yellow on yellow giving ideas
that the sun is expected

again tomorrow; as dark
holding something tight, secure

a nest of dark wrapping
in the glowing places a song

that will be sung at a time
when the singer is ready

10

to grasp a new leaf
it is endless

taking the green stalk
and holding it

warming it in hand
at breast, arms around

almost a creature
to be nursed back

but the severed stem
finds language, a waving

the cutting comes slowly
in a silent sorrow of hurt

looking into trees

refusing to see faces
(impossible in this wind
this moment)
there in the vacancies
the spaces of seconds
the crazy or controlled
crossings of green place
the flashed-out leaves
make a dizzy wall
before our eyes

go wind, go green,
go move it
into great
and greater shiftings

every year I celebrate

every year I celebrate
in this field,
full daisy high
bulked up
with blooming clover
and the weight
of grasses
the field
grows, dies
grows again
its shapes
in time
for celebration

there is so much,
the wide swath
of it turning to Atlantic
and its place
with the wide
sky picture

to throw myself
face down, full length
in the middle
of it, a way to go,
but there might
be a field-sparrow's
nest, a bobolink's

better to wait
better to wait

Gatineau summer

1

the summer was spent in the hills.
I hid in the craters. cheek against
the oldest rock. the ear listened
for the drama of childhood. the same
hemlocks. I felt for the sun.
out of the unnatural forest dark.
I sent a scream over the waters.
the first black moment.

2

older. numbers are for counting.
into age the snake makes its
promised return. at least it is
a bleak sign of movement
but why? and to where?

3

you will return to your playhouse
among the pines. there is room
to turn around. to undress.
to nudge into sleep. prayers lift.
dreams lift. there is a lift, too,
of rain cloud over the river.

4

come softly. my dark is your dark.
the bird nestles after song. through
the tissue of birch woods the words
bring smells. light unfurls banners.
life's fantastic festival of prat falls.

escape

August, it could be October;
it could be anywhere the green
of summer has bled away,
it is that kind of season,

so there was too much rain,
not enough this and everything
you can whistle up to list,
the time turns slowly, softly.

But slowly, softly are not my way,
this hooting place is dying;
there is a hope gone bad
and I root out blankets for sleeping.

there are four

I

the place is given, given over
to this rage of cloud, lights
changing in the run of it

out of the weather-west, wise
do I stand in the presence
of a high hemlock growing there

and to it all my mind measures
the long tongues of your love
rasping the mind into the body's place

go, go, some voice reaches me
and I, for one, reach alone for rain
for new following weather, your coming,

this must be it, no more finals,
the contest of age leaks its meanings,
coughs its close presence, coughs,

then to view the clearing, flying stars
write sagas over the wet dark
and you, this time, finger my lips

II

the green plants fill my room
taking moisture, storing it on glass
and what grows is silent

do you think, I ask my love,
that anything we might move to
would be such as this, as quiet?

the flags lie twisted on their poles
the place we first talked about
is heavy with living juice

your answer shrills, at least, to me
over thousands of mock-miles, giving
a torture of distant consolation

give, give, what precious stones you have,
they can be words, plain words as polished gems
a solitary yes, on hand-made paper,

the cavern echoes, the spook-bird croaks
the wild hermit is given to bursting
the pale of your YES I read at last.

III

go to it, the drunken angels dip down
their coated tongues and rock my sleep
I listen and whack them from my bed

give, give, I telegraph the trees to tell
you in your pacific place, your Kootenays,
wherever you take your western place

how do I yield, death is still a story told,
the mind rehearses, the body stiffens,
and the face folds in practised grief

what can I tell, prove once more, to you
given my body's willing place
and what you know it has already said

to it, to you, the limbered body
flies in a great albatross of curve
crashing in a splash-down of watery feathers

and I wait in the dipper-dawn
for your crash boat, your crazy crew
to lift me, lift me free.

IV

there are faces, past and present,
remembered and seen in sudden places
and they are the sullen witnesses

once I went to make my apologies
one by one before them all, and I,
in the mist of tears knew not one

but in the days after I met them
swimming on a tidal sea, each
was one, the mighty past, as swimmers

the sea was their embrace not mine
and the tidal leavings told nothing
taking all our past with it somewhere

no, I will not give up. sorry so,
the past is pushed behind, a mighty stroke,
then comes back pushing all faces closer,

higher, and what waves saw us
I do not know, but it was orgy
body to body until the tide took over.

it will have to be

and about the past
the argument dribbles on
the past is important
(count the historians,
they must mean something)

so much of me has gone
so much of me is

the feet go one before the other
there is only the sound
the beat of the past

what of now?
I cough and the future
becomes a sick-bay,
a locked room
of no entry or escape.

death, where is thy string?
to tie me up
find a good butcher
he knows the proper knots.

sun deliberate
wide flaming wings
to suffocate

to blow life,
to stifle

all at the same time
He did come
and blood-bowed
He did go

what is in between
so important
all-embracing
all consuming

God give free
with any direction(s)
for me

sinners sleep
I am one
where do I sleep
more important,
how?

the birds

stood in a rain-wash of wind
packed down in a sudden fury.
the gale picked from the sea pitch
beach where stones rolled, waves struck

wallow of music; a broken shell
fixes the eye, another, the frenzy
sends shafts of echoes closer
and beach is tossed, gone right, gone wrong

III

1

A dead house to begin with. Broken body
with empty eyes. Or so it seems. The dead
have left their barn boots, their party shoes.
Except for the frame and the brick chimney
holding all together, the rest has been smashed,
broken in. Trespassed. The passion of local
destruction is on every sullied wall, on every
leaning floor, ready to break from every bare-
strutted ceiling. Why? I spent hours under
the soured apple wind-lost trees. A lilac bush
gone wilder. To rape, to kick, nothing else,
was the Friday night game. I rant. To bring
it back, alone, this telling, working prayer-
backed place. I would begin with the hallowed
dead to see a floundered self. I shall sit for days.

2

There is enough simply on the outside.
Simply? I talk to myself in hopes that I
will be heard. The scales of shingles go in
their softening time. Nails give in. The anatomy
is unveiled. The world's morgue. Front and
across the dirt road, then to sloping fields
the red bay holds. The tidal breath is deep,
relaxing the hidden ribs of warped and smooth
flats. The sensuous curves lie moving I know,
but are undetectable. There is so much inside
us in the same condition. Cumberland Basin
looks back on this old hack of house. Let me
spend more nights, more days crouching, voiceless,
confused by old prayers, no joy but the deep
tremor within me. The rude limbs of lilacs
pierce through leather. A sign? I would die.
For a song. Give me words.

3

You give it all. All to it. To the
falling away and building. Prayers come in
pieces. My fingers split and shake. It is dark,
too dark for blood. There are changes in me.
Already my certain limbs go brittle. Leaning
against the broken door I stand, hands raised,
shouting. Who hears? Stars wait. Owls
burrow in the upstairs rooms. They pass in and
out like strange bees. The soul is in the midst
of rout and debauch. The rude eagled-past flies
through me in knocking waves. I limp around
this old garden carrying a mangled thing. To
fall now is to give in. My knees bleed. To
praise.

4

Cock morning at Upper Rockport. Peck's
Cove, Peck's Point. I know the signal of the
strangled bird. One of the few. I am not sure how
I feel. The woods out back now have my first
trails. Real feelers. I am to begin. Always it
is this. Flags of prayers flap in the wind of
my head breathing their own suggestions. They
mean nothing. What am I to say standing here at
a hollow window with my stretched arms seeking
one word? Just one. Something to begin my songs
and psalms of questions and of praise. I follow
the noises of birds. What is all this around me?
Love may come through a crack. This fund of
green, yellow and red. There is much to be made
of such colours. The seasons provide wide hints.
Even these escape me on this beyond morning of my
unsure and weeping soul.

5

All night questions lay in my throat. They
took up my vitals. Waited in my mouth like
fishes in a bucket. They are for asking. Some
curl and cough to death within me. Others grow
out of their bones and flesh, take on the same
scales. I am told there are questions for me
to answer. I am my own inquisitor. But I need
your tossing brawn, your courage coursing through
me to form answers. Answers I will believe and
not escape from. They are all yours after all.
Perhaps I am going about this the wrong way. Who
is to know? Another question. Only the rock I
found in the broken place behind. How often do
I go to embrace it? To lean against it. To sit
with it in the beginning morning when mists grow
wide over the red water. There are horses then,
ghostly horses fleeing and returning. How they
move around this rock.

6

Who slept here? In this collapsed bedroom
there were eyes that opened, legs that moved.
Dolls of the past. There are stories in jig-
saw. Somewhere files hold names and numbers. The
house moves with life. It is not dead. This is my
discovery. This is my own telling. I am not dead.
There are breathing things. They crowd around
and would smother. I escape down the few stairs.
It is something, all of this, which shatters. Do
I bleed too much? Make it all a stage to parade
clowns in ragged coats. In prat-fall folly for
my private theatre of laughing surfaces. Underneath
is where I am heading. This is all a staggered
dream. Is it?

7

A finding. A miracle of dried-up apple.
I hold it up to the light. Lights from some
magic diamond. How do the eyes cope? I
shut them and listen. A song moves. There is no
back-up. Alone the song becomes mine. The
words come from a wizened fruit. Child from a
past of orchards. Through a message of blossoms,
the kiss of perfume in this old and dying place.
Already I forget. It is alive. I spend hours
making a musical instrument. It will never
speak. There are only the words. I hear them.
What invisible linnet finds my ear? My rage is
lost. I find fields for singing. May they
take me in.

8

Someone in the night. It is black. The
air is heavy with old scents of people, vegetables
gone bad, logs rotting in tumbled graves hidden
in grass. There is a face here. Now. I pull
open a nailed cupboard I have been afraid to
touch. There is noise of movement below. I
want to speak to the moving visitor. Someone.
Someone to listen and to accept my repentance.
This is the whole frenzied exercise. It came in
an instant. This is the parlour. No furniture.
I talk into the dark. Are you a messenger?
Do not go until you hear my ragged chapters.
Treat me as a child whoever you are. I said
much until my soul was dry. Whoever was here
has gone. Of this I am certain. I seek for
eyes.

9

Suffering is common. It is a sharing. How
do I walk out of this place? My past omissions
weigh me down. To walk along the Wood Point
Road. But I think this way because the visitor
has gone. Before that coming I was not alone.
Under every rock, inside every weed, is your
remarkable beauty. I am beginning to see it
now. Now there is less suffering. I want to
stay. I sit in the kitchen window. Glass
gone. Frames wrenched out. There is a
silent strength in this old place. I will crawl
in the back fields at night to trap the
visitors. I will ask for mercy.

10

It is slow work over an uneven land.
In old grass and furrows I make my closet-
nest. Strategies begin to fill my moves.
They are so obvious I feel defeat already.
What will happen with all of this planning?
Soon someone will come. It will all be easier.
Even a few words will do wonders. But will
you be watching, listening to all of this?
It is a cold field on a cold night. Words can be
like fires, flames around the heart. No, there
will be no encounter. My suffering has only
begun. Perhaps when I have stripped myself of
the past's worms I will move closer. At least
we are talking. The dead house is my temple-
cover.

11

These last days. Moments stretched. Reaching. More
voices. Dream praises against a black field.
This is the tricky part. Danger-time. Am I as I
the really vulnerable? My soul stays. Phoenix.
Fires burn. This is the centre.
In the parlour the fireplace has been torn away.
Signs of brick. Fieldstone. Whatever was there?
A new decor for praise. This is the way I want it.
To suffer is to begin. The only way.
No invention here of an ideal landscape.
No, this is the place. The soul lifts.
From here.

12

A dream's dormitory. Faces hang like balloons.
Over a wide field. Above the house
the air is a sprawl. Tumble-cloud. I tremble
at the hanging place. The window gives way
to light. Moving now is a crawl of cloud
from north somewhere. In the corner
torment grows in my hands. In the dream-
assembly, I too find myself in a dark wood.
The time is mid-life. A festival of new fears.
What did I see, just then? Sleep brings
its own lights and shadows. Now there
is colour. This is the inferno part! The pulse
tells.

13

Beyond the low roll of fields a strewn disaster
of ice-blocks on the winter's basin. Brown stew
from a giant stomach. A god's breakfast.
Bad joke. Feeling of morning. What was said?
I look back at the night's broken play.
Again, there was something moving. New
tracks move from the house. To reclaim
the night. Nursing in bursts of fear.
I remember eyes. The brush of uncommon hair.
Moisture from a shimmering presence.
By the far ice there is movement. Dreams.
Tracks. A cougar slants its way. To trees.
Was this the wet-eyed presence? I hollow out
a place to wait. Shell-scrape. To watch.
To listen. Just as warnings shout from tombstones
down the road.

14

In my knocking guilt I address a sudden multitude.
Heads of thousands. Looking up the plague of faces
grinds and changes. Eyes become trembling, exotic,
fanning birds. It is a tumult. Over the grasses,
embracing the apple trees, they cover the road
and fill the fields as far as the water. Wet
and shining. Sea soaked. Dragged ashore.
The house is a swaying mansion gone sour.
'Let us give thanks for the four angels of the winds.'
The crowd laughs and chants their names.
The mass has something to do. From the upstairs
window I hear *Raphael! Uriel! Michael!*
Gabriel! Directions are confused. Are these
thousands a stampede of evil angels? Are
the watchers frozen because they slept with women?
the stadium begins to empty. I awake in a deserted
place. Limp grass from naked feet.
Where are the uncertain watchers? Do
morning stars still sing together?

15

Around this place I am my own Virgil. Geography.
  Profile.
I finger it across one wall. Plaster intact. Hairs in it.
At the head of the front stair. I am tempted
to use circles. The old chestnut with man
at the centre. Blake's calipers. Each room
is a kneeling place. I weep.
All acts are over. Yet there is laughter
of a wild boy. Louder than I have
ever heard. It is mine. This is comforting.
Just as this house is heaven and hell.
Grand and simple design.
Room takes to room. Hallways. Front
and back stairs. What else is round?
Frozen apples. The sun reaching in from
Peck's Point. More rectangles of light.
I must place things in order. It is
a deep and savage way. It will be mine.

16

The map possesses me. Who needs it? Dust
or snow will blow it clean by morning.
Is this, for me, the woeful city? Is this
the dripping ground of eternal grief,
the groping lost? Is there an inscription
over the kitchen door? *Abandon hope.*
Questions grow as ribs of day. No waiting
for answers. I shake with the swaying
house. The retching fields. Cracking
trees out back. My map reads like
arctic snow. Who is to take its drifting
messages? Now, in the collapsing dark
I fall somewhere.

17

Time to touch. Fingers on old boards.
A stage of broken things. Plaster smashes
against walls. There are devils' songs.
The wind plays a part. My ears blur
between cymbals. What is left? More
feeling. Old nails and splinters.
Daytime is framed by fire. The invisible
guardians touch back. There is warmth
I do not need. Knees make my penance
play itself out. At least for now. A
damage of crows over the outside
fields. Noise takes. A falling.
Next room.

18

Sin shakes from a neon dream. I am
too old for bed and war. There is only
the stumble into the past's long catalogue.
I shrink from stricken sentences of love.
'You have changed' and I fall from a hammock
in Outremont. Only others were lechers.
I lie face-down in a quag of wires.
A self-made net of old sallies. Quick
nonsense of hurting loves. The haunt continues.
Wires tighten. A maze burns in each eye.
The room is lined with scribbled accounts
of each fall. So many. Really? Out there
a spill of plover at the tamarack point.

19

Demon day. Right on for the race of inner wrath.
Who else burns? Questions shake and flop
on the wind. Bottled silence. Windows
and doors. Boarded up. Devils are carpenters.
Battle contained. Now flames blow through
cracks in the night. Afraid to move. A strange
warmth. There is only one real fire. Love, the
fire of it. What is it doing in my pocket? The
strain of hours clicks like a timer. No
answers here. A glimmer in the cracks.
The shrine of it sticks.

20

Face into face. Wild reckonings. Oedipus.
Whose part? From the living room
I spin-roll onto grass. It is sudden.
Fire burns and I reach for it in my hair,
breast, legs. No flame.
A dip of hell. My grovel attracts
a noise of crazy choruses. Past faces.
No play with sweetness. Charity. Love.
Faces are masks. Masks are faces.
The crazy logic turns in the senses.
This is still the inferno part.
Is there a twitching hole? Escape
from all this?

21

Dawn. Squint light. Dream fragments.
Window. East. The window is first shape.
Ducking into shadows. Waking. The stage
is a splintered heap of beams. Old pine
hauled over scrub fields. Sap and sweat.
Shouldered end to end. Not much.
Enough. A comedy of sounds. A flare
of robins. Chorus to begin. A fragment
stays. A leaf of love falls like a straggler.
Wader off course. Something new.

22

I carve my own passage. Posters lurch
in white corridors. Statements of light.
I listen for the tongue's valour. Who
is trumpet-tongued? Are these
the night's dark agents? Now is fire.
Black smoke in the same shafts.
Then I fell. Pain talk is private.
Old confetti of plaster. Who hid
the banister? Reel in a drawing-room
of past gods. The reckoning continues
down old drains in my own voice.

23

Surprise of quiet. Here. Now. Despair.
The eyes I look for but cannot see. Morning after.
Again. You know I am spiritually insecure.
Know it. And you too, bedad.
Pain peculiar. Ride of blood over the world.
Angels caught in it. Oil slick birds.
Pray for downpours. In from Basin.
They kneel clawing air. Blake's winds
draw us together. My life is ahead.
No problem. Pluck wild figs. The answer
is to live it. Come up.

24

Working visions. Establish my goings.
Sports of old mights. Thin sights down
tired dreams. Parade of faces. I would sleep
with your smile. Was old. Old bones
and forget your roaring. No, I would rather
sleep and die that way. Your lips
are the beginning. We tangle as lovers.
There is thunder inside. We let each other out.
Limp selves. Wobble tracks in old snow.

25

The first horizon. New cloud-flesh.
A world-place. Our eyes dash
to soft places. This creaking basket of love.
Float over new waves. Basin warm
as blood. Now, locked stilts of fingers.
A surprise you are. Memory is dead.
Window-frames flare as gold. Highlights
of nipples. Smooth rounds. Lip and tongue.
Start golden bride.

26

To establish my goings. Set them straight.
Paint valour on my tongue. The future
(forget last night) in the instant. I must
go and do more temple-haunting.
There can still be strong knots of love.
From the clammy heights of yesterday.
Next stop in the edge of the valley.
Moss grows in crevasses like death.
Deep damnation. You are your worst.

27

This is my wax of roaring. Dreams and clouds
make desperate yards. Only crazed agents
have my number. Here. I am looking out.
Trumpet-tied before the Lord. Out of breath.
Now in this broken place and season
I stumble on a mad map of my cloistered flight.
Open a brown bag. Blow it up. Insanity
in celebration. I heap hands of strange
new wonder. Peck's Cove remains.
A warm safety. Dance at low tide.
A plunge at high. New traces over
Cumberland basin. There. Look from here.

28

Coils of light. Drunken tracers. Measures
are being taken. Bracket target. There's
a good boy. Past of a packet of sound.
Ears play new chords. Cordite in belches.
No replay. Old sights take on laughter.
Smells and a running thunder of sound.
Senses reel in a twist of feet. Recoil.
The map points to a backing up. There
is a hoedown in the living room at dawn.
Fiddles fly. New dances pull the walls in.
Line-up. Not alone. Floor-nails pop
from stomped-on sockets.

29

Hidden help of cloud. A run of it.
Everyday is morning. Whipped hemlocks
as distant pavilions. All motion of sea.
Starting place. All day dance. Non-stop
devotions. No repeats. Knees spent from kneeling.
Who has heard any part of this?
House of weird spinning. Remember the party shoes.
There in the window. Laces taken.
Needed elsewhere. The golden sun-up
unties a signal. Another.

30

Burst again. Set-yellow sun. Picks up
the Basin. Happy wind out there.
Broken walls take on wondrous shadows.
Great halls. Stairways lean into warmth
and loveliness. Domestic. Only to stare.
Past of imagination and groping memory.
New celebration. Starburst of shingles
on the front facade. Far out along
the ledges Peck's Point is strong. There
is growing everywhere. I take it.

The text of this book is set in Goudy Oldstyle and printed
by the Tribune Press on Byronic Recycled paper in an
edition of 500 copies.
The title ornament is based on a form from the Boston
Type and Stereotype Catalog (1832) as reproduced in the
Dover Pictorial Archives series.